My Silent Demise: An Honest Account of Life With Anorexia

Julia Miller

BookLeaf Publishing

Presentation by *BookLeaf Publishing*

Web: www.bookleafpub.com

E-mail: info@bookleafpub.com

ISBN: 9789357440950

First edition 2023

DEDICATION

to my roommate.

i will always love you.

ACKNOWLEDGEMENT

I wouldn't be sitting here piecing together this series of poems if it weren't for Dr. Catherine Miller. When it felt like no one else truly understood, she guided me through weekly weights, inpatient stays, meal plans, and residential programs. More than a decade later, I have her to thank for the bits and pieces of recovery I've maintained over the years.

Katie- the person who has named my children, FED my children, held my hand through NICU stays, answered my frantic texts about various legal matters, and most importantly, encouraged me to always stay with recovery- I wouldn't be able to do it without your snark, your ever-so-dry sense of humor, and your biting honesty. (See what I did there?) Thank you.

Mom, Dad, and the never-ending list of siblings: from day 1, you've been there; driving back and forth to Stanford and Menlo Park, from Oregon to Utah and everywhere in between. Thank you for putting up with this disease and for getting me help when I needed it.

Papa. I will never forget the chemistry lessons on the inpatient ward at Stanford, getting 'scoops' at Cosentino's, the Lollipop song on the way to the cabin, falling asleep on your lap during WWII documentaries, or the way you always say 'Oh,

Julia...' when I give you good news. Everywhere we went, it was apparent that you touched people's lives in a remarkable way- from the bagger at the store to the janitor at the hospital. My papa knew them and had made a difference. But most of all, you've continued to make a difference in my life and I will undoubtedly appreciate you and how much you mean to me until I cease to exist.

To my twin- you know who you are. I'd get a thousand seemingly inappropriate tattoos with you any day. I promise to always keep my word when I tell you that I will be able to safely drive home at the end of the night.

Rich: my brother from another mother. I know I'm cool, but you didn't have to steal my birthday.

To Kimm, Sezy, Steph (#biteclub) Cory, Eudie, Ian, Amy, and all the countless supportive and influential people I've met over the years. I am increasingly grateful for each and every one of you.

PREFACE

Anorexia is a deceitful, debilitating disease that kills tens of thousands of people per year and otherwise severely disrupts the quality of life for those who are still suffering. It spares no race, no age, and no gender. Anorexia doesn't care if you have a family to raise or if you are mid-coursework attempting to obtain a degree. It will wreak havoc on every aspect of your life and it won't stop there- it strips you of your physical health, your mental wellbeing, your social interactions and relationships, and eventually, your life. I write to expose the secrets we are forced to keep. Maybe then, those with eating disorders can be understood, treated, and healed.

I Didn't Want to Feel This Way Again

Time slows
and with heavy limbs
I wade through the
fear and dread
that surround me.

Despair hovers and
anxiety lurks,
as I rapidly descend
into a dark cavern
of lethargy and confusion.

A skeletal feeling
suffuses my face
and the weakness sets in
as I adjust to this
familiar refuge.

I didn't want to feel
this way again,
but now that I'm here,
I realize how much
I missed it.

Without Warning

it might seem
like a distant memory,
but in all reality-
it's always watching,
impatiently waiting
for life to feel
the least bit overwhelming;
and you think you're healed
so you skip a meal,
then shit gets real,
and you begin to question your sanity.

Relapse

Tortured by these demons,
their talons rooted in my soul-
deepening,
twisting,
tightening,
a grasp I can't control.

An identity once left behind
now sits right beside-
haunting,
taunting,
tormenting,
a duplicitous face, it hides.

These thoughts, they consume me,
further deranging with every bite-
gnawing,
nagging,
devouring,
any remaining sanity denied.

A merciless disease that infects
the mind, the body, and the soul-
infiltrating,
permeating,
overtaking,
leaving a gaping hole.

Everything I Can

Surviving on loud music
and bad decisions-
doing everything I can
to keep my head up

Above the water,

I can finally breathe;
freed from this suffocating cloud-
doing everything I can
so that I don't get buried

Underneath the weight

of this avalanche,
I lose myself-
and do everything I can
to ground myself

As I land on my feet,

I connect to the beauty
around me-
and do everything I can
not to get sucked down

Into this tornado I go,

swirled around endlessly,
losing control-
doing everything I can
to stay afloat.

Here

i am still here-
all but my consciousness:
a voiceless vessel,
a silent spectre,
a stereo without sound.

Did the Power Go Out?

A breaker's tripped,
can't find the switch;
a clutch that won't engage.

It's a fulltime gig,
plus overtime,
just to heal this brain of mine.

Press Play to Begin

I want to see the beauty
instead of all the pain
and if I could just wake up
I could start to live again

It's Not A Choice, I Promise

I stare at the hollow remnants
of what I used to be
as I pass by the mirror and wonder
what took my personality.

Now before you ask,
"Why don't you just eat?"
It's really never that simple-
something is stopping me.

No motivation to nourish,
to flourish, or thrive.
I've lost any innate ability
to keep myself alive.

It's not me, I promise,
although it's my choice to change.
This monster is haunting me;
I'm locked in a cage.

Some say a prison of my own making,
a self-imposed hell.
I didn't choose to starve myself.
I want to be well.

Hungry for More

The insatiable desire
for something to complete me;
something to make me feel
more than this hollow shell
of a human being-
shrinking,
disappearing,
wasting away.

A hunger for fullness
not even food can provide.

It's Not About the Food

"But you've always been skinny!"

"You could never be fat."

It's not about the food or my weight. When will you understand that?

Running Towards Fear

Each meal is like a marathon,
except instead of my feet
pounding the pavement,
I'm lifting a fork that
bears the weight of my soul.

As my thoughts race,
panic and doubt consume me.

Not Sick Enough

You're not sick enough
unless your lips are chapped
and you have hair
on your face.
You're not sick enough
unless you can see your ribs
and your heart
has slowed it's pace.

You're not sick enough
unless your hair falls out
and your blood
won't circulate.
You're not sick enough
unless your labs are affected
and your vitals
won't compensate.

Ridiculous Food Rules

These five foods are the ones that are safe,
but you must freeze them first.
Only eat when you can barely function,
and drink when you're dying of thirst.

Go to bed hungry,
Don't eat before noon-
this will ensure that you don't eat too soon
and risk going over the two times permitted.
Any "weird parts" must be omitted:
rip them off, cut it up;
it's better if you eat really slow.
You're limited to Gatorade-
only the red and white kind though.

Did I mention that your already limited selection
now only comes in these specific flavors?
Use your left hand.
Don't forget a fork.
Always leave some on your plate.
Oh, and by the way, that big dish? Off limits.
And you're not allowed to savor.

Don't worry about keeping track of it all,
because tomorrow everything will change.
I'll keep feeding you lies
and these rules- expanded and modified;
each one more and more deranged.

Fat is Not a Feeling

"Fat is not a feeling,"
but when I'm full,
all I feel is rage.
Crawling out of my skin,
I need to escape
from within this treacherous cage.

It's not the eating that scares me,
or even the specific food.
It's the guilt and the shame
and the sadness and rage
that I know I will feel
when I do.

A Promise Believed But Never Kept

"I can't lose any more weight. If I do, I will die."

"You can, and you will. It will be different this time."

Facing My Mortality

Coming face to face
with mortality is
like staring up at a
mountain I'm expected to climb
but sliding downhill
at the very same time.

A Disease of Contradictions

I want so badly to be full of life,
yet strive to be void of emotion.
I gain the strength to go on,
and then get too weak to function.

I crave all the food around me,
but can't get myself to consume it.
I have a thousand reasons why,
but always want to quit.

I want to fade away
and be seen at the very same time.
I have no reason to live,
but I don't want to die.

This is Your Brain on Anorexia

a glitch.
a malfunction.
complete dissociation.

coded 404: file not found.
input does not compute.

quick to forget.
slow to react.
reasoning skills are less than intact.

Glascow Score: low.
unable to focus.
possible altered mental status.

can't think straight.
blank state.
nothing is making sense.

no signal.
head in the clouds.
playing with an incomplete deck.

memory loss.
an absent reflex.
a disconnect in the prefrontal cortex.

The Unexplainable Force

A force field surrounds me.
I just want to cry.

"Take the first bite."

I can't.
It won't let me and won't tell me why.

Nothing makes sense.
My mind, without thought.

"Eat now, feel later."

If I do, it will know, and then I'll be caught.

Tell my family I love them.
Please tell them I fought.

"One bite at a time."

Easy for you to say. It's harder than you think.

I Gained Weight

I gained weight,
my cycle is on track,
my hair regrew,
and my vision is back.

I can smell things now,
I'm not always cold,
my muscles don't cramp,
and I don't look too old.

My wounds heal quickly,
my lips aren't always dry;
so if my body is thriving,
why can't my thoughts comply?

Two Voices

There are two voices inside of my head:
one so desperately trying to keep me alive,
and one that wants me dead.

But before it kills me
it will strip me of my dignity
and all that I hold dear-
it will start with my identity, my family, and then
my strength.
Any normalcy I thought I had will all just
disappear.

It will take my hair,
the color in my cheeks,
and then my vision.
Not to mention my ability to stay warm
and my overall cognition.

It will prevent me from caring for my kids
or even driving-
anything it can possibly do to
keep me barely surviving.

My mental health is next to go,
along with my sleep,

my appetite,
and even Aunt Flo.

And even then, it still isn't done-
there goes my teeth,
my hearing,
and bone density 'til I have none.

It will rob me of my capacity to make decisions
for myself
and any chance of fighting infection.
Then it goes on to continue
it's devious abjection.

Any zest for life,
motivation,
or creativity I had left
is all snatched up
in it's evil plot
to destroy my life through theft.

It takes and takes,
leaving me broken and alone.
Pretty soon all that's left will be
just a gravestone.